Confession Can Change Your Life

David Knight

Nihil Obstat: Rev. Hilarion Kistner, O.F.M.
　　　　　 Rev. John J. Jennings

Imprimi Potest: Rev. Jeremy Harrington, O.F.M.
　　　　　 Provincial

Imprimatur: †James H. Garland, V.G.
　　　　　 Archdiocese of Cincinnati
　　　　　 November 19, 1984

The *nihil obstat* and *imprimatur* are a declaration that a book or pamphlet is considered to be free from doctrinal or moral error. It is not implied that those who have granted the *nihil obstat* and *imprimatur* agree with the contents, opinions or statements expressed.

Scripture texts used in this work are taken from the *New American Bible*, copyright © 1970 by the Confraternity of Christian Doctrine, Washington, D.C., and are used by permission of the copyright owner. All rights reserved.

Book design and cover by Julie Lonneman.

SBN 0-86716-041-1

CONTENTS

Introduction: Looking at Confession—
And What It *Can* Be   1

Chapter 1: Focusing on Reconciliation—
And Four Changes in Our Approach
to Confession   9

Chapter 2: Reforming Our Lives—
And Why Confession Hasn't
Seemed to Work   15

Chapter 3: Taking Confession Seriously—
Public Confession in the Early Church   21

Chapter 4: Confessing Privately—
Historical Developments and Today's
Expectations   25

Chapter 5: Taking the Magic Out—
And Putting the Community Back In   32

Chapter 6: Emphasizing Community—
And Four Ways to Make Confession Work   37

Chapter 7: Judging Our 'Fruits' Not Our 'Sins'—
A New Perspective on Conscience   45

Chapter 8: Affirming the Incarnation—
Why We Confess to a Priest   52

Looking at Confession— And What It *Can* Be

VATICAN II USUALLY gets the credit—or the blame— for most of the changes in modern Catholic life. In some instances, however, changes have taken place which Vatican II had no desire to foster. One of these is the decline in individual confessions. People just aren't going to confession the way they used to.

It is commonplace today for priests to hear, "It has been a year (or two years, or five years) since my last confession." Such an admission used to be the identification code of a lost sheep returning to the fold. Now it says more about the state of the Church in general than about the individual person.

Priests are also noticing the phenomenon of the "second postponed confession"—young people in grade school or high school who confide that they have never been to confession at all since the first time they received the sacrament. Clearly attitudes have changed.

In 1983 the Synod of Bishops met in Rome to discuss pastoral questions connected with the Sacrament of Reconciliation. They too remarked on the decline in individual, private confessions. As a key element in this decline the bishops pinpointed the absence in today's society—in Europe and North America at least—of an authentic sense of sin, and noted that unless people have a feeling of personal disloyalty toward a personal, loving

God, the Sacrament of Reconciliation will hardly attract them.

As Cardinal Joseph L. Bernardin, then Archbishop of Chicago, speaking at the Synod put it:

> Penance is necessarily rooted in a sense of personal sin. Faith in Jesus Christ gives us access to the Father; it makes possible an ever-deepening grasp of God's power, love and holiness. But with this comes a growing sense of sin, whose full weight is visible in the crucified Jesus. We see sin, furthermore, in personal terms: as evil for which we are morally responsible. Our sorrow is therefore equally personal: "I have sinned against you whom I should love above all things."

So the problem today is more than people not going to confession. In many cases they are not confessing their sins to a priest because they are not admitting their sins to themselves. They may cite, in justification of this, the principle, "It is enough to confess my sins to God alone." But underlying their confusion about the role of the ministerial priesthood in the Church as a whole is another confusion about what is and is not serious sin in their own, personal lives.

Going into the Synod, the American bishops issued this statement:

> We believe that the present state of affairs points to a widespread confusion on a number of basic questions: the nature of sin, personal moral responsibility, the meaning of "fundamental option" or life-orientation as a factor in personal morality, the role of Penance in spiritual growth and maturity, and the nature of the sacramental system within our sacramental Church.

The Synod focused the attention of the Church on the real problem: The pastoral question about Reconciliation has less to do with *confession* than it does with *conscience*. Before people accept the *role of the sacrament* in their lives they have to admit the *reality of sin*. If the sacramental rite of Reconciliation is properly renewed, however, this can help straighten out the theological confusion.

ACTUALLY, IT MAY BE a good thing that people are confused about just what is and is not "mortal sin." For the fact is that anyone who is not confused about mortal sin in the Church today really does not understand the situation.

Teaching methods and pastoral practices before Vatican II gave people the impression that the identification of mortal sin was a very simple procedure. Catechisms gave lists of mortal sins. Anyone who was adequately instructed and not crazy and who consciously did one of these things was presumed to have had "sufficient knowledge and full consent of the will," and was going to hell in a handbasket unless he or she made it to confession before death.

This approach made things simple. And, in spite of the terrible guilt feelings some veteran Catholics recall, it made things relatively easy. So many apparently inescapable actions were "mortal sin" that you picked up the idea it really wasn't all that important to *avoid* mortal sin; the important thing was to get to confession before you *died* in it. This made for lots of business in the confessional and a steady, but not very enlightened, pressure for reform.

What we have today is very little pressure for reform, and not much enlightenment either. But at least we have recognized confusion. And as Archbishop Szoka of Detroit quipped in the Synod: *"Vexatio dat intellectum"* ("Irritation leads to understanding"). The more a problem bothers us, the harder we will work toward its solution.

The fact is, it is not always easy to determine just when one has (or has not) committed mortal sin. And it never was! True, we used to teach clear rules to children.

And we always told the scrupulous, "Don't worry. If you commit a mortal sin, you will know it." But a lot of reality is too complex to explain to children. And what may have been a valid principle for the scrupulous (since real sinning and real knowing have little to do with the anxieties they deal with) can be misleading for ordinary people whose consciences are not so convoluted. The problem of serious guilt is just not that simple. To try to make it simple can lead to the self-condemnation of scrupulosity, the self-righteousness of pharisaism or other forms of self-deception.

The Church does recognize some actions as seriously wrong—and to know that the Church considers something seriously wrong is enough to alert a believing conscience. But when someone chooses to do one of these things regardless, it is not always easy to judge just how much personal, subjective guilt there is.

It is possible to have "sufficient knowledge" to *call* something a mortal sin without having sufficient knowledge to commit it as a mortal sin. We have to take into consideration here such questions as the maturity of the individual, real knowledge as opposed to just "head" knowledge, and personal appreciation of how wrong something is as opposed to just having been told how wrong it is. In other words, actions which may be objectively serious sin in themselves may not be subjectively and personally *acts* of mortal sin for the person who commits them.

Take a high school boy speeding down the street, for example. Does he really have "sufficient knowledge" of how dangerous this is to be guilty of mortal sin? If the same boy should happen to kill someone, however, he would know the danger of speeding on an entirely different level of understanding.

It is probably a good thing that Catholics are not as quick as they used to be to say they have committed mortal sin. Mortal sin is death to the soul, and it is not something one gets into or out of easily. Quick and easy confession can have the effect of making deadly sin and radical restoration to life also appear quick and easy, which just isn't true to life.

THE KNIFE CUTS both ways, however. If it is damaging to judge one's guilt too harshly, it is also damaging not to judge one's guilt realistically enough. To say there is no sin where there is sin can lead to the deadliest sin of all.

Suppose someone is sinning and rationalizing. There may be sufficient lack of real knowledge to keep guilt from being mortal. But the sin itself is going to have its effect. The combination of sin and rationalization, if it persists, can take all taste out of the spiritual life, make faith seem unreal and lead to the abandonment of religion altogether.

When people in this situation stop going to Mass, for example, they usually will not say it is because they have sinned, but rather because Christianity has become meaningless or the Church community seems alien to them. And this is the truth—because their sin has made it so. One cannot live in objective contradiction to the teaching of Jesus Christ and feel comfortable hearing his teaching proclaimed in church. A strong enough rationalization can keep the contradiction from being conscious, but it cannot keep it from being felt at some level. When one is not living according to faith, every celebration of faith tends to become a "downer" ranging from meaningless to positively repugnant. And the Christian community, instead of being a source of support, is a torture to be around.

Those, then, who are not subjectively in their own consciences guilty of mortal sin, but who are doing something seriously sinful in itself, may be dangerously close to a decision which will turn their whole lives away from God. When this decision becomes a fact, then we have a choice that is truly mortal. This is "deadly" sin, sin that kills the life of grace. The chances of this sin being confessed in any immediate time frame are very slim.

The scariest thing about this picture is that when sin has become subjectively and personally mortal it is least likely to be noticed. It is logical to deduce that those who have in fact lost the life of grace will no longer have the spiritual perception to recognize the fact.

So we can see that it is no simple thing to know whether one is or is not in mortal sin. The deadliest thing about sin—any sin—is that it blinds as it kills. Long before one's sin has become mortal it is more than likely that one's spiritual perception has become dulled. Thus, anyone who consistently engages in actions contrary to the objective moral teaching of the Church would be wise to entertain some healthy doubts about the subjective life and safety of his or her soul.

This is where frequent, private confession can play a valuable role. Instead of frequent confession being based on the recurring need to receive absolution for mortal sins, it can be used instead as a sacrament for the prevention of mortal sin and for the continuing clarification and purification of mind and heart. This is what, historically, the Sacrament of Reconciliation evolved into in the Catholic Church. And this is what I believe it can and ought to be for the practicing Catholic today.

The Sacrament of Reconciliation, then, is a medicinal sacrament. It has the power to restore life when the life of grace is lost. But it also has the power to prevent the loss of this life, to save people from getting—unknowingly—so deep into sin that they wind up losing the faith and leaving the Church. The sacrament can also foster growth in the spiritual life through the ongoing clarification of ideals and the continuing conversion of the heart toward Jesus Christ.

THIS IS THE REAL FOCUS of this book: that the Sacrament of Reconciliation is one of the most powerful—or potentially most powerful—instruments in the Church for *personal spiritual growth* and *continuing conversion of life*.

Pope John Paul II pointed this out as he prepared the bishops for the Synod: "The Sacrament of Confession," he wrote, "is the irreplaceable means of conversion and spiritual progress." And later, in his closing address to the Synod, he told the bishops that in his encyclical *Dives in Misericordia* the "most important passages are dedicated to the problem of *metanoia*, that is to say, of penance as conversion, or rather continuous conversion toward God." Reconciliation, the Pope continues, "is the fruit of this conversion." Taken together, "penance (*metanoia*) and reconciliation reveal themselves as a dimension, indeed the fundamental dimension, of the entire Christian existence."

Used this way, as a tool for continuing spiritual conversion, the Sacrament of Reconciliation takes on an important place in Catholic life. Confession can not only restore life; it can also give new vigor to the life of grace and direct it to further growth.

Reconciliation is a sacrament of change. No matter how good or how bad the person may be who uses it, confession calls for deeper conversion. And this is a conversion toward the fullness of life (see John 10:10).

Life, conversion and change should be our goal and focus in the Sacrament of Reconciliation. So let us now explore how confession *can* change your life.

CHAPTER 1

Focusing on Reconciliation—
And Four Changes in Our Approach to
Confession

EVER THINK ABOUT the morning after in the Story of
the Prodigal Son? The boy is forgiven, he is restored to the
good graces of his father, the celebration has been held
and the fatted calf is a pleasant memory.

Then what?

To end the story with the father's forgiveness of his
son is to leave out half the reality. There was a lot more to
the boy's leaving than just an abstract offense against his
father. A whole network of relationships with other
people had been broken off or altered. A lot of confidence
was shaken. People who thought they knew the boy
before he left home found out that they didn't really, or
that he had changed. When he came home, they weren't
sure how to relate to him. There was reconciling to do.

Reconciliation means that relationships are clarified
and accepted again. People explain to one another where
they stand, who they really are, what their past actions say
or do not say about their present state of mind, their true
orientation of heart and will. To be reconciled with
another is to feel you know that person again; you know
what to expect of the other, what you can count on.

There's a big difference between forgiveness and
reconciliation. The Church recognizes this, and is
speaking of confession today more and more in terms of
reconciliation. This doesn't make it any less a sacrament of

forgiveness, but if we see confession as a ritual merely to obtain God's forgiveness, our picture is not only incomplete but distorted.

To see forgiveness of sin just as the act of being restored to the good graces of a previously angry God—as if God will punish us if we do not get right with him again through sincere repentance and this religious ritual—is to understand sin and repentance, forgiveness and reconciliation in a pre-Christian way.

JESUS CHANGED all that. Because of Jesus and his redeeming life, death and resurrection we are in an entirely different relationship with God. God is not for Christians the angry God the pagans knew and feared, or feared because they did not know him. When we sin, we do not have to win forgiveness from him by placating his offended majesty with sacrifices or satisfying his aroused justice with penitential practices and prayers. God is our loving Father. He waits for us with anxious care before we ever turn back to him, while we are "still a long way off." The moment he sees us coming toward him again he is deeply moved. He runs out to meet us, throws his arms around us, and kisses us (see Luke 15:11-32).

The prodigal son didn't even have time to tell all his sins—to make what we call an "integral confession." Before he could finish the little speech of apology he had prepared, the father interrupted him, called for a robe and a ring, and told the servants to bring on the fatted calf. His forgiveness was never even in question. This is the way Jesus describes the Father.

As for God the Son, he is our Savior, not our Judge (John 8:15). He is on our side. He came to earth precisely to "search out and save what was lost" (Luke 19:10). He is the Good Shepherd, laying down his life for the sheep (John 10:11), leaving the 99 to follow the lost one until he finds it (Luke 15:4). And when he finds it, he "puts it on his shoulders in jubilation" (15:5). What he wants is to restore the sheep to the fold, not to keep it at a distance. Not to punish us for sin, but to fight for us and with us against the sin which is our common enemy.

And when we recall that the name given to the Holy Spirit—the Paraclete, or Advocate—means the same as (although much more than) "lawyer," we begin to get the picture. Suppose you had prepared your legal defense for days with your lawyer, wondering who the judge would be and how you could expect him to hear your case. Then when you finally got to court you found that your lawyer had been appointed judge, while remaining at the same time your lawyer! Well, the Holy Spirit, who has been sent by the Father and Son to speak for us, to be at our side and counsel us, is one God with the Father and the Son. Our Judge, our Savior and our Advocate are all one and the same!

The intention of the Gospels is to deliver us from that fear of an angry God and that worry about God's attitude toward us which weighed on pagan minds. It is not the forgiveness of God we have to be primarily concerned about once we are in Christ Jesus; it is reconciliation with our brothers and sisters.

Our great commandment is not justice, but love. We fail God most deeply as Christians when we fail to be for one another what we are gathered together to be in love.

That is why our sins—our shortfalls—cry out not only for forgiveness from God but for reconciliation among ourselves. Sin doesn't just create a need in the individual for forgiveness; sin creates a need in the Body of Christ itself, in the Church as a whole, for reconciliation and a restoration of relationships. It is not just a matter of restoring the sinner to God's friendship, but of restoring the wholeness of the Body of Christ. Wounds have to be healed, lines of communication repaired, confidence reestablished, bonds of understanding and love strengthened, the life of the Body quickened, the work of witness carried forward. What we have taken away from the Body by our sin, we have to restore to the Body through our repentance—and through the expression of that repentance to the community of believers.

This puts confession—the Sacrament of Reconciliation—in a whole new light. Confession is not a matter of going into a secret little closet as an enemy of God, fearful that one is under sentence of eternal death, and coming out a friend of God with a certified ticket to heaven. What drives us to confession is not primarily fear of God's anger and punishment but, rather, love of the Body of Christ and concern for the community we have damaged. Does one apologize to one's closest friend out of fear, or out of concern for the relationship that one's actions may have damaged?

IF WE ACCEPT THIS new understanding of ourselves, of sin and of the real implications of repentance, then four things should change in our basic approach to confession:

1) *We should approach the Sacrament of Reconciliation with less concern about being forgiven and with much more concern about repairing the damage we have done to the community of believers.* We must focus on restoring the bonds of unity, mutual confidence and love that have been weakened by our conduct. And to make this real we should look to what our sins have done—and even more to what they have said—to those who are closest to us: our family, our friends, associates at work, fellow parishioners, other Christians and nonbelievers.

2) *We should be much less concerned about keeping our sins secret and much more concerned about making our repentance known.* I am not suggesting public confession of sin, of course; any sin that is secret should be kept secret. But

most of the sins people confess are perfectly well known to everybody who lives with them. What others do not know, quite often, is how we ourselves feel about our sins, how we judge them. Our sins say to all who know us that we don't care about some truth, some value. Repentance says that we do care. To confess our sins is to profess our faith, and this is the real point of the sacrament. We confess sin as sin to show that we sincerely do profess the attitudes and values of Christ as true and real. To say that we were wrong—and know that we were wrong—is to say at the same time that Jesus is right, that we believe and accept the way of life he teaches.

The Sacrament of Reconciliation is a way of repairing the damage we have done to the community of the Church, the false witness we have borne to Christ. We who are believers and disciples of Jesus Christ have acted in a way that is not true to his teachings. This puts Christianity—Christ himself—in a false light. So we confess that we were not expressing the truth of the Church or even of our own deeper ideals in what we did. Confession is a way of re-declaring to the Church, and to those who are closest to us, who we really are, what we really believe in, what we are sincerely trying to live up to.

The confession of sin is a profession of return and concern: of *return* if we have left or broken with the community of the faithful by actions incompatible with the profession of Christ; of *concern* if we have shown a lack of concern for values we previously professed in faith.

In any case, the value of confession lies not in what is kept secret, but in what is made known, namely, the truth and reality of our ideals. For this reason, when the sins we have committed are public knowledge anyway, there is no value in keeping secret what we are repenting of. It would be much better if those closest to us, at least, might know for what we are asking God's forgiveness and theirs.

3) *We should not let guilt feelings narrow the focus of our attention to the wrong things we have done but rather, in the spirit of the gospel, approach confession with a sense of responsibility for the good we ought to be doing.* The aim of the sacrament, after all, is growth; and spiritual growth is largely a matter of changing our mind about something we didn't see before. The scriptural name for this change of mind is *metanoia*: sometimes translated "conversion," and sometimes translated "repentance." The more we understand what we are called to be, the more we repent of what we still remain. The closer we come to the light of Christ, the more we realize how much in the darkness we were prior to each new moment of realization. What the Sacrament of Reconciliation is all about is seeing more clearly where we fall short and determining more decisively how we are going to live.

4) *We should do away with the exclusive individuality of our preparation.* We are used to examining our consciences in private. But in any other area of life if we want to know where we are falling short, we ask someone for an objective opinion. This is beneficial, not only to alert us to external faults, but also to help us identify our deeper attitudes. Why shouldn't we ask others, who live or work or deal with us, to help us pinpoint the reasons why grace does not bear the fruit it should in our daily lives?

The role of the Christian community (on whatever level it exists—priest, parish, family or friends) is crucial in helping us use confession as a means to continuous conversion of mind and heart and will. By each one of us converting again and again to a closer identification with the attitudes and values of Jesus Christ, and doing this with the aid and knowledge of the Christian community, we become more and more reconciled with each other in that loving "unity which has the Spirit as its origin and peace as its binding force" (Ephesians 4:3).

CHAPTER 2

Reforming Our Lives—
And Why Confession Hasn't Seemed to
Work

PUT YOURSELF IN the priest's place on a typical parish confession night. An anonymous male voice behind the grille intones, "Bless me, Father, it has been about a month since my last confession." You register: "Just a month—a regular—probably a pretty conscientious Catholic." The voice continues: "Since my last confession I've been impatient with my wife a few times—probably my fault. We've had some arguments. I've told lies on maybe four or five occasions: nothing big, but I know it wasn't right. I've had too much to drink on maybe two occasions. I try to watch my language, but I've slipped a few times. And I'm probably not as good a father as I should be to my children. I mean I don't spend the time with them that I ought to, and I yell at them sometimes. I guess that's about all. For these and all my sins I am heartily sorry."

If you were the priest, what would you say? A pretty routine confession. Who doesn't get impatient, cuss a little, drink a little too much at times? At least the man seems concerned about it. He needs encouragement, realization of God's love for him. So you say some positive words, suggest he say a few Hail Mary's for a penance (or if you are a little more theological as a confessor, you might suggest he do something to make up for his faults, like bringing his wife flowers some night), and you give absolution. Close the grille, next penitent.

The next voice behind the grille is a woman's. "Listen, Father," she says, "the man who just walked out of here is my husband. Now I know you can't tell me what he said, but I can tell you what he said!" She then proceeds to give a pretty accurate summary of what her husband's confession was.

"He probably told you he had 'a little too much to drink on a couple of occasions,' right? Well, the truth is he has too much to drink on every occasion—every night, every day, every week. The two times he was speaking of were two weekends when he was so bombed out of his mind he didn't know what city he was in. Our kids have never known him except in one of two moods: the happy, party-time poppa and the hung over grouch. We don't communicate; his head is always in the clouds or under an icepack.

"Then once a month he betakes himself to confession and gets all his guilt feelings out. And one of you clowns (all due respect to the priesthood—how could you know any better?) pats him on the back and tells him he's shiny clean again, and he's Mister Magnificent for about two days. If I get another bouquet of flowers from that guy, I'm going to burn the rectory down.

"Our marriage is on the rocks. Our kids have emotional problems; I wouldn't be surprised if they all left the Church just as soon as they get out of the house. But my husband won't face the truth. He just goes to confession every month and then everything is free and clear. You call that a sacrament of reconciliation? You call that a sacrament of healing? This sacrament is destroying my home!"

THE POINT OF THE STORY is that the picture the man paints of himself in confession does not in any sense portray the real condition of his soul or the reality of his life as a Christian husband and father. And so the priest's response to him in confession has results that are exactly the opposite of what they should be.

Instead of helping the man, confession is giving him just enough emotional release from his guilt feelings to keep him from ever facing or doing anything about his real problem, his real sin. Every time this man begins to feel guilty and depressed over the kind of husband, father and man that he is, he can go into the confessional, turn himself in for trial before a judge who is already instructed to be sympathetic with the compassion of Christ's own heart, and present the case against himself in private with the assurance that no other witness for the prosecution will be allowed. He knows from experience that it is a rare priest who will take up the office of inquisitor; most priests place themselves affectively on the side of the accused and try to make the person feel better. So this man will go out from his session of self-accusation relieved momentarily of his guilt feelings, and falsely reassured that in the eyes of God everything is all right again in his life.

In reality nothing is all right. Everything is all wrong. But he doesn't know it (or isn't facing it) and the priest doesn't know it either. The only ones who know it are his wife, his children, all of his close friends, his business associates and a miscellaneous cross section of the general public. In other words, everyone knows it except the only two people the Church can rely upon sacramentally to do something about it: the priest and the penitent.

This is one of the reasons why confession is bearing so little fruit in the Church.

IRONICALLY, THERE is probably no sacrament in the Church more specifically designed than Reconciliation to help a person respond to the most fundamental preaching of the gospel message: "Reform your lives, for the Kingdom of God is at hand." But the tragic irony is that

17

confession has come to be quite consistently used—in reality abused—to reassure people, in contradiction to the gospel, that no serious reform of their lives is necessary.

How many priests could stand up and bear witness that the one thing they almost never encounter in the regular hearing of confessions is a genuine conversion experience! (When I say "almost never" I do not exclude the one or two instances on a given occasion that really made the sacrament an experience of restoring life.)

In other words, Catholics in confession are seldom experiencing, expressing or even expected to be expressing a real act of repentance, of *metanoia*, a real decision to change and reform something significant in their lives. Most confessions are just reiterations of the attitudes and values the penitent has always held. People slip—they fall—into sin and they confess it. There is no conversion. In most cases the fall was just that—a stumbling along the way without any real change of course—and the repentance is no change either. The person's attitude toward a particular sin *after* confession is no deeper or different than before having committed it or confessed it.

No one is particularly proud, for example, of being impatient with his wife or kids. So everyone confesses it and keeps doing it, because everyone believes this is the kind of sin no one can really avoid. It seldom occurs to Catholics that there is a *cause* for impatience, at least for constant or recurring impatience, and that the cause should be systematically sought out, confessed and removed from one's life.

Catholics seldom advert to the truth that patience, peace, love and joy are fruits of the Holy Spirit (Galatians 5:22), which means their absence points to a falling short in a person's Christian life. And what is true of such a common fault as impatience is true of all other faults: Where a fault exists a cause exists. And that cause—more so than the fault itself, most likely—is the real matter for confession.

If a husband and wife do not have a deeply satisfying marriage characterized by love, peace, joy and a real growth in the spiritual life of their children, there is a cause for that. And that cause should be sought out and brought to confession. If an individual cannot shake off a deep bitterness over the changes that have taken place in the Church, or an impenetrable prejudice toward persons of other races, there is a cause for that. It is a sign of something missing in the way one is living the life of grace. That cause should be discovered and brought to repentance. And repentance means that the cause itself should be removed from one's life, at whatever cost.

In other words, the Sacrament of Reconciliation should deal with unearthing and rooting out. In confession the ax should be laid to the roots, and every branch that is not bearing fruit should be cut out or its connection reestablished with the source of life and fruitfulness, Jesus Christ (Matthew 3:10; John 15:4-7). Confession is an act of making the crooked ways straight and the rough ways smooth for the coming-ever-nearer of Christ the Lord into the heartland of our choices, our attitudes, our values, our lives of personal response.

THE OPTION OF face-to-face confession, introduced several years ago, encourages such an in-depth confrontation with one's real sinfulness. This method allows for a more natural dialogue about the entire direction of one's spiritual life—as opposed to just a litany of offenses. The whole atmosphere encourages openness and healing and growth, rather than secrecy and shame.

For confession should deal with reform—with the kind of repentance (*metanoia*) that realizes the true meaning of the word: conversion, a change of mind, the acceptance of a higher value, of a different attitude in faith, in the light of which we can begin to see that our previous conduct has been falling short of the gospel ideal.

The root meaning of the word for sin in Hebrew is "to miss the mark," to fall short. Sin for a Christian does not mean to do something bad; it means to fall short of the good that one should be realizing in one's life. For a person to sin against Christian marriage, for example, it is not necessary to be unfaithful to one's spouse. It is enough just not to communicate deeply with one's spouse; not to be able to pray naturally and spontaneously together with one's husband, wife and children; not to be personally involved in, responsible for and effective at making one's home a truly Christian environment, a milieu where one's children can grow in deep, personal experience of God and appreciation for the faith.

This is the area confession should deal with: reform of life until one reaches a fullness of Christian living, a fullness of life in faith, hope and love. But this is not what confession has dealt with in our experience, and not what we have become accustomed to expect it to deal with.

Confession as we experience it deals with forgiveness, not with reform; its concern is the taking away of sin, not conversion of mind and heart. It is a car wash, not an overhaul. We use confession like a toothbrush when we should use it like a dentist's drill. We keep brushing off the surface of our lives while the interior is being eaten away with decay. We are like chronic overeaters who go on periodic diets without ever getting down to changing our basic eating habits.

How did we get this way? There are many reasons, of course. We will look at some of those reasons in the following chapters.

CHAPTER 3

Taking Conversion Seriously— Public Confession in the Early Church

WE CATHOLICS HAVE to remind ourselves that confession as we know it came about in the Church only through a process of evolution which spanned several centuries. Public, not private, confession was the norm for the first 600 years of Christianity. It was not until the sixth century that private confession began in Spain, spread to Ireland and, through Irish monks, to the continent.

Up until the ninth century, when the Church began to ease up, strict penances were imposed, designed to prove the sincerity of the penitent's conversion and to purify whatever evil within had led to or resulted from the sin. The penance imposed might include fasting, going without sleep, wearing a special penitential costume in public (sackcloth and ashes, for example), abstaining from marital relations or even giving up one's trade (in which case the Christian community was expected to support the penitent with alms as well as with prayers). The penance imposed might last for a period of months, or for anywhere from five to 20 years. Sometimes a man might be required to do penance for the rest of his life—to abstain from sexual relations with his spouse, for example, or give up his means of livelihood forever. And absolution was not given until after the period of penance was completed, whether this meant waiting for years or even not receiving absolution until the penitent was actually at

21

the point of death.

We stand aghast today at the thought of such a discipline of penance. It seems almost more barbaric than Christian. But we have to understand why it seemed to the people of that time to be the normal thing to do.

The early Christians were very conscious that Christianity should be a total conversion of mind and heart to Christ. The grace of Baptism, the grace of Christ, was the gift of new life—a life that brought with it the power of the Holy Spirit to live on another plane of existence. The Christian was one who had died to life as it is spontaneously lived in this world, and who had been reborn to live in every respect as a member of the Body of Jesus Christ. One did not become a Christian in the very early days without weighing and accepting the prospect of physical martyrdom. And even if one was not actually killed for believing, the fact of becoming a Christian often meant automatic exclusion from one's family, rejection by friends, and loss of material possessions, social position or political status.

What moved the first Christians to make such sacrifices and make them joyously was the gift they experienced of new life in Christ—the gift of a transformation of attitudes, of a new way of looking at things. The Christians knew that the grace of Jesus Christ had enlightened their minds and moved their hearts to understand values they had never appreciated or even dreamed of before. This is what enabled them to live on a whole new plane of behavior.

They experienced in their life the fruits of the Holy Spirit: joy, peace and love above all, accompanied by patience, kindness, generosity, faith, mildness and chaste self-control (cf. Galatians 5:22). They knew that something new, something wonderful and powerful had entered their lives as a result of their decision to accept the Word of God and ask for the grace to be reborn as a member of the

Body of Jesus Christ. The gift of the Holy Spirit was a tangible reality of their experience.

The person of Jesus Christ was also an experienced reality to them: They knew that henceforth they had accepted Jesus, the incarnate Word of God, as the Way of life, the Truth of life, the very Life that gave meaning and ultimate value to the life they were born with.

In the light of this the early Christian saw serious sin—mortal sin—as a deep, deadly decision to abandon the way of Christ and return to the way of the world. One didn't pop in and out of accepting and rejecting Christ. The idea of being converted from sin, going back to it, turning back to Christ, returning again to sin, only to be converted again back to Christ was to the early Christian a contradiction in terms.

IF WE THINK A BIT, we will realize that it is just as much a contradiction today. People do not pop in and out of mortal sin. If they are repeatedly committing adultery, for example (which is certainly the serious matter required for mortal sin), then we should presume one of two things: Either they are subjectively so unaware of the seriousness of what they are doing, or rendered so unfree by passion and deep psychological needs, that they are not subjectively guilty of committing mortal sin with sufficient knowledge and full consent of the will. Or they are not truly repentant when they go to confession and, regardless of the absolution given by the priest, their sin is not forgiven.

It is not within our purpose—or our capability—to judge here which of these two alternatives is the more general reality in our day. We do not presume to judge (and no one can) whether a particular person is committing mortal sin and not being absolved from it, or whether the individual, for subjective reasons, is not personally guilty of mortal sin at all. The point we are

23

making is that one either is truly converted to Christ, truly renewed by his grace, or one is not.

We are talking about basic life-options here; the fundamental orientation of one's life is something that does not easily change. No one accepts Jesus Christ as Lord and God one day, and forgets all about him to chase some passing creaturely gratification the next day, and then turns painlessly back to Christ the following day by saying a few words in the confessional.

This is what the first Christians recognized very clearly. They knew more in this respect about human psychology than we seem to. If a person, after being converted to Christ, fell into serious, explicit sin, they did not presume it would be easy to turn back to Christ again. Either the sinner had not converted deeply and authentically the first time, and thus the sinner's word was not to be taken very seriously, or else the sinner had truly converted to Christ, had truly rejected him and would not truly be converted back without some doing.

The first Christians emphasized reform of life, deep repentance of sin and acts of penance as proof of the sincerity and strength of perseverance behind one's profession of conversion. The rite of sacramental Reconciliation was for them the fire in which the gold is tested and purified. And the man or woman who went through the rite of penance and absolution knew he or she had been through something significant and had come out of it a different person.

All of this is a bit idealized, of course. Nothing in human life ever takes place exactly the way it is supposed to take place in theory. But the way the early Christians practiced confession shows, at least, how they thought of this sacrament and what they presumed it was supposed to accomplish.

What, by contrast, do we think of it? What do modern Catholics expect confession to accomplish in their lives?

CHAPTER 4

Confessing Privately—
Historical Developments and Today's
Expectations

WHAT DO CATHOLICS today expect confession to accomplish? As we said in Chapter 1, Catholics look to confession for forgiveness. If Catholics do something wrong, they want some assurance—a guarantee really—that God has forgiven them. Very often what they really want even more than the assurance of God's forgiveness is the assurance that they are not going to go to hell for their sins. This might sound like the same thing, but it is not at all the same thing in the reality of the penitent's psychological and spiritual attitudes.

If I am going to confession out of fear, fear of otherwise being punished for my sins by some stern and vengeful God, then what really interests me in confession is not what effect my confession has on me, but what effect it has on God. I am really not concerned very much about what kind of state I am in as a person (a husband, father, wife, mother, employer, employee, citizen, believer). What I want to know is what kind of state God is in. Is he angry with me? Is he going to throw me into hell if I die? I want to be in the state of grace because that is synonymous, in the context, with having a certified ticket good for one reserved seat in heaven. The "state of grace" is something God will honor and accept on Judgment Day.

This attitude toward confession differs very little, if at all, from the attitude with which a guilt-ridden native in the jungle would approach a witch doctor. Confession so understood and practiced is basically an act of magic; it is engaged in as a guaranteed means of manipulating God. Absolution provides a talisman against the infinite unknown of the deity's power. It is not so much a human act which expresses and engages the mind and heart of the penitent as it is a semi-magical act which changes the attitude of God.

It is my fear that this understanding of confession may be encouraged, even inculcated, by the way we practice private confession today. In order that I might not be misunderstood, let me insist from the outset that I think private confession is potentially one of the most powerful, most helpful practices of the spiritual life. I am in favor of private confession—provided confession in private is used as it should be, with full awareness of what it is, what it is not and what it must not be allowed to become. It must not be allowed to become just an easy out from guilt feelings in a person's life (as it was for the man in Chapter 2 with the drinking problem), a way to put off indefinitely facing seriously what is keeping one from really living like a Christian.

SO LET US LOOK at what private confession was in its beginnings. Private confession was essentially a process of conversion, a form of spiritual direction. It was used by people—both monks and laity—bent on serious personal reform and growth in the life of grace. In confession a concerned Christian sought advice about his or her spiritual condition, and the person's spiritual adviser (who may or may not have been a priest) imposed the kind of penance that would help the individual overcome whatever vices or deficiencies were blocking spiritual progress. The penances were long and arduous, geared to reform of life. In this stage of its development, the emphasis in the reconciliation process was on a deep, interior change of heart, on conversion and contrition.

But when this kind of confession became commonplace in Catholic life, it began to be used by a large percentage of people who had little idea what conversion or spiritual growth were all about. Confession soon lost the character of serious conversion of life and shrank to a sin-shriving formality, at least for many people. Gradually the penances were reduced to a mere formality too—three Hail Mary's if you were good, a rosary or two if you were bad. And soon confession became what we know it to be today.

And so confession came full circle. In the first days of the Church the emphasis in the sacrament was on public satisfaction: convincing the community by public penance of the sincerity of one's repentance and faith. In the Middle Ages the accent was more on interior, personal contrition and conversion of heart. Later the main focus switched to the actual confession of sins and the absolution given by the priest.

To understand and use the Sacrament of Reconciliation authentically, however, all three of these elements must receive their full value: Interior contrition and conversion must be real; the bond of trust and fellowship with the community must be restored; and reconciliation must be accomplished in the sacramental confession and absolution of sins.

In recent times, however, the first two of these elements began to be seriously neglected. Even so, confession remained and remains a powerful sacrament for many, many persons, a fruitful medium of encounter with the living God. The grace of Christ works with power regardless of circumstances, and there is no question about the spiritual effectiveness of regular confession, even when the handicaps are heavy.

But the fact remains that, along with the working of the Holy Spirit in the heart during confession, along with the encounter with Jesus Christ embodied in and acting through the priest, along with the outpouring of the Father's love on every prodigal son or daughter who sought reconciliation through confession, another reality established itself: the implicit concept of confession as being just a process established for the removal of personal guilt in private. The real focus was on absolution. And as Cardinal Bernardin pointed out in the Synod, "exclusive focus upon the moment of absolution without appropriate attention to the previous journey of conversion opens the door to a magical view of the sacrament."

To put the focus too exclusively on absolution not only drops personal conversion and penance into the background, it also tends to drop the Christian community out of the picture. Even though in reality the priest in absolving always speaks for the bishop and for the community—and in this way speaks for God—still, private confession has come to be experienced as a secret encounter between the penitent and God, with the priest acting as intermediary.

The idea was obscured and all but lost that confession is also a transaction between the individual penitent and the rest of the Christian community. The notion that individual Christians are accountable to their fellow believers for the way they give (or do not give) public expression to their faith was practically lost. The priest's role as judge, not only in the name of God, but also in the name of the community, was likewise lost. Priest and penitent alike tended more and more to reduce the priest's responsibility and function to that of giving absolution, in which he was seen to be speaking for God, and for God alone.

THE CONFESSION SCENARIO that accompanied this overemphasis on absolution went something like this:

Penitents were confessing their sins to God, through the medium of the priest. The priest was there to relay God's forgiveness to the penitents unless something was obviously deficient in the penitent's disposition. The priest did not presume to ask many questions, or any questions at all, unless they were absolutely necessary. The whole idea was for the penitents to say to God what was burdening their souls, to blurt out or whisper whatever they had to say, and for this to be made as easy for them as possible. Thus, penitents were not explaining themselves or accounting for their conduct to the Christian community or to the priest; they were simply mentioning all of their sins—and the emphasis was on getting them all out there on the counter, not omitting any—so that the priest, in the name of God, could wipe them all away. Any sin not mentioned was not wiped away (unless it was forgotten). If any unmentioned sin was remembered later, it had to be put onto the counter in a later confession.

This self-revelation was presumed to be embarrassing and difficult (a presumption that was usually exaggerated or not warranted at all). For the priest to make it more embarrassing by asking questions was to make the sacrament distasteful or, in the language of pastoral theology, "odious," which was to be avoided at all costs. The idea was to make it easy for all of the people to get all of the sins out so that they could all be taken away and nothing would remain unconfessed to send a person to hell at the moment of death.

Absolute secrecy was (and is) guaranteed so that no one would have any excuses or insurmountable difficulty about making an integral confession. To keep anything back in confession was about the worst thing a person could do. The very secrecy of the confession encounter—a wise and merciful secrecy—reinforced the idea that confession was really a transaction between God and the individual soul, with the priest acting as God's personal representative, a mere functionary empowered in the sacrament to grant forgiveness binding on God.

It is enlightening to notice the role sexual sins began to play in this context. The whole aura of secrecy preconditioned the penitent to expect confession to be something embarrassing: the secret revelation in a dark closet of things experienced as shameful, things too embarrassing to talk about face to face. Children were assured that the priest would not even know who was talking and that in any case he could never reveal to anybody anything told in confession. For most children, and most adults, about the only things for which they would want such assurance of secrecy would be sexual sins and murder: sexual sins because of what the priest might think of them, murder because of what society might do to them if the truth leaked out. Since most people were not committing murder very often, this tended to give the confessional box the affective coloring of a secret little closet in which one whispered about sex or other things felt to be equally shameful. Even what was not shameful seemed to feel shameful in confession!

It is perhaps significant, in confirmation of this, that just about the only sins that ever seemed to present any problem in terms of reform of life—any problem about receiving absolution or the validity of absolution given— were sins involving sex. Adolescents with habits of masturbation, married couples practicing birth control, someone involved in an illicit love affair—all tended to stay away from confession on the assumption that they could not have a sincere purpose of amendment. In some cases the priest might even have denied someone absolution for one of these things unless there was a promise to stop doing whatever one was doing.

Other sins didn't have the same priority in confession as sexual sins. Sins not surrounded with any feeling of shamefulness didn't seem to count as much. People were rarely, if ever, denied absolution because of racial prejudice, for example. (One good reason for this was that people rarely, if ever, thought to mention racial prejudice as a sin.) Business and politics hardly came up in confession. Perhaps these were considered ethical decisions rather than moral ones, just as the word *immorality* in popular language is spontaneously taken to refer to sexual misbehavior unless otherwise qualified. Whatever the reasons, sexual sins seemed to be the biggest thing one had to be worried about in confession, and about the only thing that might keep a person from absolution or Communion if one did not reform. I believe that the whole aura of secrecy that surrounded confession had a lot to do with this.

CHAPTER 5

Taking the Magic Out—
And Putting the Community Back In

THE PRACTICE OF private or secret confession excluded the Christian community physically and visibly from the action that took place in confession. But in reality the Sacrament of Reconciliation is not just a transaction between penitent and God with the priest in the middle. It is a transaction between an individual and God with the Christian community in the middle.

Christ gave the power to forgive sins to the Church. The appropriate person to exercise this power is the bishop, because the bishop is the official head of the local Church. (The priest, of course, can speak in the bishop's name in this.) The bishop can forgive sins not only in the name of God but in the name of the Christian community, because he is the official, recognized spokesman for the community. And so it is in the name of God and of the community that the bishop receives back those who by sin have separated themselves from Christ and from the community of believers.

Just as Baptism forgives sin by incorporating a person into the Body of Christ, so confession forgives sin by being a visible re-incorporation, a re-integration, into the Christian assembly.

Through sin we do not totally cease to be members of the Body of Christ. But if our sin is deadly—that is, "mortal"—we cease to be live members in full, vital

contact with other members and with the Head of the
Body, who is Christ. Every mortal sin is an act of
separating oneself from the life of the Church. It is an act
of leaving the community of believers in a very real way.

In a sense which is more truth than exaggeration,
every mortal sin is a denial of the faith. We do not by every
sin formally renounce our belief, but we do break with our
fellow believers. By freely choosing to act in a way
incompatible with the teaching of Jesus Christ, we
implicitly deny that we believe in his teaching in any real,
self-engaging way. We cease to stand together with our
fellow Christians in affirmation of the world view of Jesus
Christ.

The Church didn't really face the question of its
power to forgive sin until the problem arose of those who
denied the faith under persecution. Some Christians,
yielding to torture or fear of death, publicly renounced
Christ. When they were released from prison they were
also relieved of their fear. So when the other Christians
assembled for Eucharist, they showed up too, asking to
participate.

This provoked a crisis of credibility. The other
Christians couldn't understand why they would want to
participate: "You don't believe in Christ anymore. You
have given up being a Christian. We heard you say so!"

The answer they got was probably something like,
"Did you see the teeth on those lions? I was wrong—I
admit it. I gave in to pain and fear. But I still believe, and I
still want to follow Jesus. I am a Christian. I just sinned."

The point is that the *confession* of sin was a *profession* of
faith. If those who denied Christ had also denied that
there was anything wrong in this—denied that it made
any difference, or that Jesus had the right to expect people
to face death for him—then it would have been clear that
they did not, in fact, believe in Jesus as Lord and God. But
if they confessed their denial as sin, in this act they

reaffirmed their faith, and the path to reconciliation with the community was open.

It was open but it wasn't going to be easy. The early Christians were so conscious of the power of grace, so aware that the reception of Baptism gave new life, divine life and the strength of the Holy Spirit, that they could not understand how anyone truly reborn in Christ and truly converted to him could ever deny him—much less deny him one day and profess faith in him again the next! Christ is life, the rejection of him death, the early Christians would have said, and you don't pass in and out of life or death easily! So the released prisoners, in order to be reconciled not only to God but to their fellow believers, had to convince the rest of the community that their conversion back to Christ was sincere. And this, as we have seen, required some doing. It involved years, sometimes a lifetime, of hard, public penance.

In this whole process the person who spoke in the name of the Christian community was the bishop. He listened to the story, weighed the penitent's sincerity, decided what penance should be imposed to test and strengthen the conversion back to Christ and finally received the penitent back into the Christian community, into full participation in the sacramental, Eucharistic life of the Church. The absolution (which only the bishop gave) was just as visibly an act of re-incorporation into the Church, of re-integration into the community, as it was an act of removing sins. The absolution, like the penance and the confession itself, took place in public, in the midst of the whole Christian assembly.

THIS HISTORICAL SKETCH is greatly simplified, but in broad, general lines it paints the historical origin of sacramental confession. What the history brings out is the authentic nature of confession as a very communitarian act. Before the penitents received absolution, before they were accepted back into full membership in the community, they satsified the whole community about the depth and sincerity of their conversion to Jesus Christ. The bishop questioned them in the name of the community, imposed penances that would make their conversion credible to the community and received them back in the name of the community. There was nothing private or secret about it.

Later and very gradually over a period of centuries, Christians became conscious of more and more actions that were, in themselves, incompatible with profession of the Christian faith. Adultery and murder were ranged alongside of apostasy as acts that placed a person outside the Christian community. As time passed, the Christian people came to realize that any really deliberate, free decision to act against the teaching of Christ in a serious matter is a decision, for the time being at least, to break with Christ and his people, an implicit denial of the faith, a rupture of the bonds of communal hope and love. The need for confession and sacramental absolution was extended to every mortal sin.

Since so many of the sins recognized as mortal were private, and since public confession of them could do untold harm in many cases, the practice of private, secret confession grew up. As we have seen, this practice obscured the true nature of confession as a communal act and the nature of absolution as an act in the name of the Christian community. The bishop delegated to priests his authority to absolve and to speak in the name of the community in reconciliation of sinners. This too obscured the nature of confession and absolution as a transaction between the individual penitent and the whole community of the Church.

Confession no longer appeared as a visible, public profession of conversion from sins of which the whole community was aware. It was simply a private removal of personal, secret guilt. Less and less did the priest question, impose penance and judge the sincerity of one's conversion in the name of the community, requiring evidence of conversion that was credible to human eyes. He just absolved in the name of the God who reads the heart, relying on the penitent's awareness that any insincerity would be known to God, and that God could not be mocked.

Such an awareness might be adequate to forestall conscious, deliberate insincerity. But most of us sinners are good at bamboozling ourselves. Our deception of others is no greater than the unconscious, unrecognized deception we practice on ourselves. We rationalize, we shade things, we stick to a pretty vague and general level of accusation even in our own examinations of conscience. Anyone who has talked to prisoners in a jail or alcoholics in a ward can tell you the difference between the way the offender sees the case and the way it stands up in court in the light of objective questioning and evidence.

SO WHAT'S THE SOLUTION? That private confession should be abolished? God preserve us from that. That rigorous, public penance should be reinstated? May God have mercy on us! But that something should be done to make confession less of a purely individual, private affair between a sinner and God, with the priest a rather passive middleman in between? Yes, by all means.

CHAPTER 6

Emphasizing Community— And Four Ways to Make Confession Work

IN THE SYNOD of Bishops Cardinal Joseph L. Bernardin made what might be a very radical proposal for involving the whole Christian community in the process of reconciliation:

> I suggest that consideration be given to a new rite of Penance, modeled on the Rite of Christian Initiation of Adults. I do not propose it in place of those which now exist but as a further option which has merit of its own.
>
> The new rite would have four stages: the confession of sins, doing penance, the celebration of the sacrament, and the prolongation of the sacramental experience in the setting of the Church community.
>
> In effect, this proposal provides for reinstituting the Order of penitents of the early Church.
>
> Though initially it would no doubt be chosen only by a relatively small number, it need not necessarily be an option for an elite. Its implementation could provide opportunities for catechesis for all members of the faith community concerning the Sacrament of Penance. Furthermore, by potentially engaging the community as a whole in its celebration, it could serve as a means for making parishes more effective settings for spiritual direction and celebration of Penance according to all the rites.

Cardinal Bernardin's proposal may be put into practice someday on a national or Church-wide scale.

Meanwhile, what can we do to make our use of this sacrament more effective?

We must find a way to give the Christian community a role in the reconciliation process. And we must find a way to give the Christian community some assurance of the sincerity of each penitent's conversion in order that this reconciliation may be real.

If a man's sin is drinking to such an extent that no authentic Christian family life is possible in his home, then that man should not be able to receive the assurance of reconciliation with the Christian community from a priest until his wife has been involved in his case, and his wife and children have seen a radical reform in his behavior. If a woman's racial prejudice is making Christian community impossible or very difficult in her parish, then that woman should not be able to receive sacramental assurance of her good standing with God in the Church until she has changed her attitude and behavior in a way that publicly repairs the scandal she has been to the community of faith. It should not be left only to the individual to present the grounds which call for reconciliation. The community should have something to say about whether a person is living in a way that expresses the authentic gospel of Jesus Christ.

I don't mean that the community should be the ultimate judge, as if some kind of ecclesiastical People's Court should be set up. The bishop (or his delegate, the priest) is the only one who can judge sin in the name of the Church or can decide whether absolution should be given. But the priest should not have to make that judgment—in every case at least—without any evidence being admitted from any person other than the penitent. In other words, we must make confession an act of accountability to the Christian community as well as to the priest and God.

How can this be done? How can it not be done? I

think we must exclude any solution that simply scratches out the centuries of Christian experience within which our present confessional practice evolved. There is no question of abolishing private confession, of allowing the sacramental seal of secrecy to be violated in any manner or degree. We do not want to get into public confession of private sins or to impose crushing burdens of penance upon people. These are all lessons that history has taught us.

WHAT, THEN, CAN WE DO? Here are four ways to begin:

1) Let us recognize that very few of the sins confessed to a priest are actually secret. Most of them are very well known to everyone who lives, works or in any way interacts with the penitent enough to know the penitent as a person. Many more sins are known to at least one other person. Perhaps *we should each personally adopt a policy of not bringing our sins to the priest in confession until some kind of public confession and reparation has been made to those who have seen and suffered from those sins.* Perhaps the Church should encourage this too.

The sins we commit in our homes, for example, should be faced as sin in the presence of our family (at least the adult members), and there should be some agreement on what a truly Christian reform of life means for us. This same principle can be applied, due adjustments being made, to each level of Christian community of which a person is a part.

2) When we examine our consciences we should all take as a guiding assumption that very few people confess their real sins and that it is not very likely that we, without any help from others, are going to be exceptions. This can sound like cynicism, but I believe the overall fruits of

sacramental confession in the Church are enough to bear out the assumption. The sins that destroy individual, family or social life are not the sins which we are likely to acknowledge in ourselves or bring up in confession. The real sins are usually the rationalized sins.

Knowing this, *we should not be content just to confess individual acts of sin; we should dig deeper, seeking the cause or root sin underlying the external acts, for these may be nothing more than symptoms.* What we confess as sin is usually the fruit of our real sin, not the root at the source of our trouble. And it is our real sin—some deep, willful attitude or accepted value in the core of our heart that is contrary to the values of Christ—that we want to repent of and bring to confession.

If we have been confessing that we drink too much, for example, we should ask ourselves just what "too much" refers to in our minds, and how much drinking we are accustomed to accept as not being too much. It may be we should not presume to bring our drinking to the priest in confession until we have sat down with husband or wife (or friends or employer) and discussed just what effect they think our drinking is having on our family life, business life and social relationships. We should listen to what they think we ought to do about it.

The same policy will apply to most other sins—to all, in fact, except those which are really so secret that others do not know they are going on. And these types are rare. If there is adultery, for example, that is not known to one's spouse, it probably should not be made known to the spouse. But it should be discussed with someone who can help us get to causes and remedies. It may be we should consult a competent marriage counselor who appreciates the value of Christian marriage before we ask absolution from the Church. If the adultery is known to both parties of the marriage, then perhaps husband and wife should go to a marriage counselor together, looking for the faults on both sides that led to the infidelity, and not presuming too quickly that it was just a simple, momentary lapse of virtue.

3) We should understand very clearly that the penance imposed by the priest and accepted by us is supposed to be something that will both express and foster a real reform of life in the area of the sins confessed. *We should not settle for a token penance if the priest gives us one (like "three Hail Mary's and three Our Father's"). If the penance given won't work and we know it, we should say so. If necessary we should come prepared to suggest our own.*

If we have a drinking problem, we should not consider ourselves fully reconciled with the Church until we have, in penance, changed our drinking habits for a long enough time to give some assurance of permanence. Our penance might be to consult a professional about problem drinking, or to give up the crutch of alcohol altogether for a few years, until we have learned what life can be like without it.

If we are chronically boring or boorish to our spouse, we should not consider our reception of the Sacrament of Reconciliation complete until we have learned to talk in a way that includes listening, thinking and sensitivity. Our penance might be to make a Marriage Encounter or to read a book on fighting fair in marriage or even to take a mini-course in communication skills. If this sounds radical, the question to ask is, "How much is a happy marriage worth? How much is it worth to me to be free of a sin that is diminishing my life?"

Confession alone, with absolution, may take away the guilt of sin, but it does not take away the source of sin, nor the likelihood of our falling into it again. It is penance which does this. That is why penance is an integral part, a necessary element, of sacramental reconciliation. And that is why the penance we perform should be more than a gesture; it should be an effective means to clear up the cause of our difficulty.

It is the sin at the root of our sins—the sin seldom confessed and even more seldom remedied—that breaks up marriages and renders family life destructive to children. And so we should call the source of evil in our life by its right name: It is sin. When love, joy and peace do not characterize our life, the explanation is not just some given fact—like lack of communication, or deep personal insecurity, or tension and dissatisfaction. The real explanation is the free, deliberate sin of not doing anything about such a lack. Lack of communication, insecurity and tension are conscience matters, not because they exist, but because we are not taking adequate measures to deal with them. And when we bring our sins to confession, the penance we receive should be a lever that works us out of the deep-worn ruts of the sin that is most characteristic and lethal in our lives.

In some cases the penance might follow absolution, as is our present practice. In other cases absolution might be deferred until we have given external evidence of a sincere intention to reform our life. Or absolution might be given with the stipulation that we return to confession at stated intervals until both we and the confessor are satisfied that our conversion is a sincere and stable one. There is nothing wrong with our suggesting such a procedure to the priest. After all, in this the priest is like a doctor who can't know whether or not the medicine is working unless we speak up about whether or not we are cured.

We should be very conscious here that a truly effective penance may have to include a way to open up a whole new dimension of prayer in our lives. It may well be that a given person (I believe it is true for most persons) will not find it even remotely possible to begin leading a truly Christian life, or to build a truly Christian marriage, unless he or she takes up prayer in a serious, regular way.

Doctors do not hesitate to insist that heart patients spend anywhere from half an hour to an hour or more in daily physical exercise—under pain of death. We should encourage our confessors not to hesitate to require as much prayer as is necessary to bring us up to the level of the actual challenge in our life. The measure of prayer demanded by the gospel of Jesus Christ—demanded under pain of spiritual death—is whatever measure is necessary for a particular person to live up to the Christian responsibilities of a given state of life: "Pray that you may not be put to the test" (Mark 14:38).

How much we must pray as Christians is determined by how much we need to pray in order to live as a Christian in all the areas of life. If at certain periods of life we need to invest an hour or even more than an hour a day in prayer in order to be equal to the temptations and challenges we face as Christians, then that is how much time we are obliged to pray.

4) *We should take a new look at the assumptions we Christians bring to an examination of conscience.* Do we examine our consciences just for "sins"—understanding by this word actions that are "bad"? Or do we examine our consciences to see whether we are bearing the fruit of a Christian life?

It is significant that in the best-known Gospel description of the General Judgment, nobody who goes to hell is there for a mortal sin! "I was hungry and you gave me no food, I was thirsty and you gave me no drink. I was away from home and you gave me no welcome, naked and you gave me no clothing. I was ill and in prison and you did not come to comfort me" (Matthew 25:42-43). If we consult the books of moral theology, we find that it is all but impossible, according to the morality we have been taught, for a Christian in normal circumstances to commit a mortal sin by not feeding the hungry, clothing the naked, or visiting the sick and imprisoned. And yet Jesus uses precisely these examples as the criteria for eternal salvation or damnation in his description of the Judgment. Perhaps we should take another look at the morality we were taught.

CHAPTER 7

Judging Our 'Fruits' Not Our 'Sins'— A New Perspective on Conscience

IF WE LOOK CLOSELY into the Scriptures we find that Jesus constantly bases his judgment of a person's life, not on the sins committed, but on the fruits grace has borne in that life. "He prunes away every barren branch, but the fruitful ones he trims clean to increase their yield" (John 15:2). The man who received only one talent and did not invest it but buried it in the ground until his master's return was condemned. And yet he did nothing bad with the talent that was entrusted to him. He did not lose it. He gave it back intact.

And so with our lives: If we do nothing bad with them and nothing good, we deserve to be condemned. If we simply preserve the state of grace in ourselves, guarding it like pickles in a jar, but do not let the grace that has been given us act and bear fruit in the world, we stand condemned.

We are to be the salt of the earth, the light of the world, the leaven in the dough. If Christians do not act to witness to the message of Christ and if the bread of the world does not rise, then the Gospel tells us those inactive Christians will be cast out as unfaithful stewards of the riches entrusted to them. The salt that gives no flavor to the world is good for nothing but to be cast out and trampled on. The man and woman whose faith and love for God do not inflame the hearts of their own children, for example, have something to examine their consciences about.

WE ARE FAMILIAR with these themes from Scripture. But they rarely constitute the basis of our judgment on our lives. Because they are not the basis on which we examine our consciences before confession, there is something seriously wrong. Scripture tells us that at death Christ will judge us on how much fruit grace has borne in our lives. But we prepare for the judgment of the priest in confession—which is supposed to be a preview and a preparation for the final exam at death—by examining ourselves according to an entirely different standard. We judge ourselves on how much bad we have done, whereas Jesus is going to judge us on how much good we have done.

With this kind of mix-up taking place, we might have to expect a lot of surprises on Judgment Day. And the sobering truth is that this is exactly what Jesus has warned us to expect: "Lord, when did we see you hungry or thirsty or away from home or naked or ill or in prison?" (Matthew 25:44). In the scenes of Judgment—the separation of the sheep and the goats, the condemnation of the man who buried his talent in the ground—those condemned are surprised at their condemnation. They were preparing for judgment according to one standard, but they were actually going to be judged according to another standard. No one can rightfully plead ignorance of this, because Jesus has made it perfectly plain in the Gospel what the Judgment is going to be about. But it is just as plain that we often pay no attention to the warning he gives. And he knew we wouldn't. That is why he tries so hard to keep warning us through the words of his Gospel.

We are accustomed to examine our conscience before confession according to lists drawn up by moral theologians and devotional writers. We were given the impression that if it isn't on the list, it isn't a sin. And so sins like a willful ignorance of the Church's teaching since Vatican II, a rejection of the new liturgy, racial segregation in our cities and schools, overcrowding of prisons, political Cainism ("Am I my brother's keeper?"), superficial communication between spouses, lack of communication between parents and children, failure to seek and accept psychological counseling when necessary, material cooperation in immoral business and political activities, failure to call elected representatives to account for their stewardship, neglect of one's elderly parents or grandparents, unsafe driving habits, consumer patronage of unworthy products—these and most of the other sins that are undermining the foundations of the Kingdom of God all remain unrecognized, unrepented, unconfessed and unreconciled in this life, whether or not we have grounds to hope they will be forgiven in the next.

We must cultivate within ourselves a new consciousness that what the gospel means in calling for reform of life is not a stricter observance of the Ten Commandments. The gospel calls for a whole restructuring of one's life according to a radically new set of attitudes and values. Those attitudes and values are just as much news today as they were in the first days when Christian preaching was known as the "Good News." And the people who live by them will find today, just as in the time of the apostles, that any life embodying the Good News of Christ will be bad news for the surrounding world. Persecution is not just a possibility for the fervent Christian; it is a promise.

In other words, Christian men and women must be very conscious that the kind of morality to which a Christian is obliged is not the going morality of the surrounding culture, no matter how good that culture is. If Christians are not bearing prophetic witness to values that are in advance of the cultural values of their milieu, those Christians are not living an authentic Christian life. They have not reformed their lives according to the gospel and they have some repenting, some changing of their minds to do.

The temptation to be concrete with examples is a pressing one here. But any worthwhile example will be, by definition, so contrary to what people are accustomed to think and accept that each example would require a whole chapter of qualifications, answers to objections and justification. Nevertheless, I offer the following suggestions as nothing but leading questions for further prayer and reflection.

JESUS SAYS THAT we should turn the other cheek, go a second mile with the person who forces us to walk one, and hand over our coat as well to the person who sues us for our shirt (cf. Matthew 5:39). If these words are not rules (and they aren't), then they must be examples intended to teach us the way Jesus evaluates persons and things. Have we understood what he is trying to say and, if so, can we point to any concrete effects this is having on our lives?

The principle behind these examples is just that we should value relationship with others over any other conflicting value on earth—for example, our pride, our time, our possessions. People are more important than things. Friendship mustn't withdraw in the face of rejection. Love takes priority over getting things done.

Translated into rigid rules, this teaching doesn't work. But to make a guiding principle out of these values is to make Christ's mind our own, and to have a very practical norm by which to judge our day-to-day conduct.

How many times have we argued or fallen out with others over nothing but material things, burdens placed on our time or hurt caused to our feelings? Sometimes one has to protest, of course, but when were our objections based on truly conflicting obligations and values, and when did they just come from a false, more selfish set of priorities? How many relatives don't speak to each other anymore because of quarrels over money? How many fights in the home come from the way one person treats or mistreats another's things? How many friendships have died because someone was not able to expose the other cheek—that is, be vulnerable again—by coming back after an experience of hurt, misunderstanding or rejection?

Jesus also taught, "None of you can be my disciple if he does not renounce all his possessions" (Luke 14:33), and "No servant can serve two masters....You cannot give yourself to God and money" (Luke 16:13). Then he told the story of the rich man who went to hell because of his attitude toward the poor man (Lazarus) who lay at his doorstep.

WHAT DOES THIS TEACHING mean? Obviously we don't have to give away all our possessions in fact, but what does it mean to really renounce them from the heart? What signs are there in our lives, in our homes, that we really do not cling to any material thing? Do we serve money as a master? How often do we feel we have to have something just because it is advertised, popular, convenient or a status symbol? How often do we Christians feel uncomfortable because of the policies of the establishment we work for? How often do we feel we are not free to resist those policies because of the economic consequences? How often do we, as consumers, feel we are voting with our dollar bill for junk? How often does our buying support economic practices we consider immoral and destructive of human society? What god are we serving in some of the ways we work and buy and sell? Have we capitulated to the economic system as to a master, a god too powerful and dangerous to challenge?

49

We could ask ourselves and one another some very practical questions: "Why did I really buy that particular product? Why in that particular store? What business policy is my money supporting? What alternatives were, or are, available? Are there alternatives that should be available and are not? Why not?" Ask those questions about the last jar of peanut butter you bought, about the last loaf of bread. Look together at the family budget. How much goes for what? How much goes to sharing with the poor?

And who is Lazarus in our day? Where is our doorstep in this age of jets and Telstar? Actually, all we have to do is turn on our television set to find Lazarus at our doorstep. How often has the daily news shown us starving faces and homeless, dispossessed refugees? "I was hungry; did you give me to eat? I was homeless; did you open your borders to me?"

A final example: The apostles teach that Christian women should not braid their hair, wear gold ornaments or expensive clothing (cf. 1 Peter 3; 1 Timothy 2). These were obviously cultural symbols in their day, so much so that recent editions of the Bible translate "braided hair" as "elaborate hairstyles." So we do not take these instructions as rules for our time.

But we have to look for and respect the principle behind them. What were the apostles really getting at? Let's not talk about immodesty in dress, since that just invites argument and ridicule. Let's ask instead what our dress—for men and women—expresses. What image of yourself are you trying to project through your choice of clothes? What value system are you accepting—and voting for with your money—if you decide to follow a particular style? What set of values do you think inspired the people who designed this style? Do your friends, your dates, your family agree that your clothes do express, objectively, the image of yourself that you intend them to express?

THE EXAMINATION I have proposed is a modest beginning compared to the vast moral problems confronting the Christian conscience today. But if we start with what is easy and near at hand, we may gradually find the courage to deal with the problem of our cooperation as citizens in such sins as the oppression of minorities, illegitimate support of dictatorial foreign governments, military aid to police states that use torture as a matter of policy, the bribery of elected officials by our highest-ranking business leaders, the diffusion of pornography, sexual promiscuity, multiplying abortions, industrial pollution and ecological devastation.

The really important thing is to begin. We have to recognize that sin is an active force in the world which can be overcome only by the grace of the gospel of Jesus Christ lived out in its entirety. And I believe we are failing as a Christian people to live the gospel in a way that brings the redemption of Christ to the world. How else can we explain the fact that millions of Christians who receive Holy Communion every Sunday are having so little impact on society? How could Adolf Hitler use all the resources of a Christian Germany to invade Europe and cremate six million Jews? How can we exterminate over a million unborn babies a year by abortion? How can military dictatorships in one Catholic country after another continue to reign by torture and terrorism while the hierarchy protests in vain? How can churchgoing America be so permeated with materialism and be responsible for exporting so many materialistic values to other nations? If we are a Christian people, why are there so many poor among us? So many who live without faith, without hope, without experience of the love of God?

Our Lord said, "By their fruits you shall know them." I think it is time we thought about the corollary: "By our fruits we must judge ourselves."

CHAPTER 8

Affirming the Incarnation—
Why We Confess to a Priest

PEOPLE OFTEN ASK, "Why do I have to confess my sins to a priest?" What they are really asking is, "Why do I have to deal with God humanly? Why should I confess my sins to Jesus Christ? Why not just talk to the God who is in heaven?"

The question is not really one of confessing to God directly or indirectly. It is one of confessing to God as pure Spirit or as God-made-flesh in Jesus Christ. If Jesus were still ministering on earth in his human body, would we still say, "Why do I have to confess my sins to a man?" (Jesus was and is a man, a man who is at the same time God, but still a human being just like the rest of us.) Why would we not say then that it is enough to confess "directly" to God?

The answer is because Jesus is God. He is God-made-flesh, a God we can talk to in human words and who talks back. The humanity of Jesus does not make God more remote; it makes him closer. When the divine person of Jesus interacts with us through his body, through his human words and gestures, we are not dealing with God "indirectly." We are dealing with God humanly, with *Emmanuel* ("God-with-us").

If God had not taken flesh in Jesus Christ, the question of confession would never have come up. God would still be nothing but the infinite, all-knowing deity in heaven who sees into our hearts and knows everything we do and think before we tell him. To confess our sins to this God directly would be enough because it would be the only thing possible. There would be no other way except to speak the words in our hearts, knowing that God already knows what we are going to say, and that his answer is something we will simply have to project in faith from what we know about him and his attitude toward us. He will not answer us in human words.

BUT GOD DID BECOME human, and this Jesus still lives and acts in his Body on earth, the Church. So when we confess our sins to a priest, we are actually confessing to Jesus Christ living and listening in him. And when the priest says, "I absolve you from all of your sins," it is Jesus who is speaking.

If any ordinary man should say, "I forgive you your sins," our answer would probably be, "Well, that is very nice, and it means a great deal to me to receive your forgiveness, but actually what I want is forgiveness from God." For forgiveness that takes away sin can only be given from God. And this forgiveness can only be given on earth in human form by the one and only "Lamb of God who takes away the sins of the world."

Thus, if Jesus is not speaking in the priest, the whole transaction of confession becomes absurd—as absurd as the Mass would become if it were not Jesus who says the words of consecration over the bread and wine: "This is my Body....This is my Blood."

Christianity is an incarnational religion. Take out of Christianity the Incarnation of God in Jesus Christ and there is nothing left. Take out of the ministry of the Church the incarnate presence of Jesus Christ speaking and acting in his human Body on earth today, and that ministry as we understand and practice it does not make sense.

So do we "have to confess our sins to a priest?" We might answer this by asking, "Do we have to receive the Body and Blood of Christ physically in Communion? Why not go to God 'directly' and just ask him to come into our hearts in some spiritual way? Why be so human, so physical about it?"

The answer is that without confession to a human being, God can forgive sins, but he cannot forgive them humanly—that is, he cannot forgive them in a Christian way, which is the way of God speaking and ministering to us in human flesh.

God forgives the sins of the Buddhists, and they do not confess to Jesus Christ present in the flesh. God forgives the Hindus, and all of those who repent in their hearts in response to his invisible grace. But their interaction with God is not a human experience of encounter with the incarnate God. It is not Christianity.

Do we believe as Christians that we are not forgiven until we confess our sins to a priest? The answer is both yes and no, depending on what one means by "being forgiven."

If I commit a sin on Monday and tell God I'm sorry on Tuesday, when am I forgiven? Not on Tuesday. Not on Monday either. I am forgiven from all eternity by the God who lives in an eternal "now," and who does not forgive in space and time. God does not change. From all eternity he has forgiven me. On Tuesday I just accept that forgiveness for myself.

But suppose that someone in the time of Christ commits a sin on Monday and on Tuesday he goes up to Jesus Christ and tells him, "Lord, I have sinned; forgive me." If Jesus says to him on Tuesday, standing on a street corner in Capernaum, "Go in peace; I forgive you all of your sins," that person's sins are forgiven on Tuesday on a street corner in Capernaum. The human act of forgiveness takes place in space and in time, because it is the act of a person living in space and time—the infinite Son of God made flesh in Jesus Christ.

Unless there is a human act of encounter with God in the flesh, speaking and acting in time and space, there is no human act of forgiveness. But this is what Christianity is all about: God-made-flesh. The option of face-to-face confession in today's Church allows the priest's humanity—his facial expressions, tone of voice and gestures—to visibly demonstrate the human Christ's warmth, concern, understanding and mercy, all of which reinforces our belief that ours is a God with whom we can interact on human terms.

SO THE PRACTICE of confession brings us right down to the heart and soul of what it means to be a Christian. The bishops in the Synod saw this very clearly. They said that the decline in private confessions is linked with a real question of faith about Christianity itself. If confession is not necessary, is the Church necessary? If the Church is not necessary, is Christ necessary?

Bishop Austin Vaughan, auxiliary bishop of New York, summed up the problem for the Synod this way:

> I believe that decline in the number of confessions is also tied in with a diminished sense of need for redemption and of the need for the mediation of the Church to receive forgiveness for sin.
>
> On the first point (diminished need for redemption), I believe that this comes from a set of beliefs that are now widely accepted by Catholics at least implicitly and sometimes explicitly:
>
> 1) A presumption that everyone or almost everyone will go to heaven so that there is no danger of anyone's losing his or her soul: because of God's mercy and his divine salvific will; or because few sins are mortal sins, and it is almost impossible to commit one subjectively (since most actions that are designated as seriously wrong will not by themselves turn around a person's fundamental orientation to God).

2) The consequence is that there is no urgent need on the part of the individual for reconciliation, or for the Church, or for Christ.

This is a challenging summary of the problem, precisely because there is so much truth in it. The fact is that Catholics believe it is possible to "get to heaven" without a conscious, explicit belief in the Church or in Jesus Christ. We believe in "baptism of desire" and in the existence of "anonymous Christians" who, like the pagan Magi on their way to Bethlehem, are coming to Jesus with truly grace-inspired faith, but while following a "star" of their own religion. These people are being saved and their sins forgiven without any conscious, human interaction with God-made-flesh in Jesus Christ, and without any human interaction with his Body on earth, the Church.

The problem summarized by Bishop Vaughan will probably preoccupy—and enrich—the Church for years to come. As theologians ponder and believers pray (hopefully united in the same persons!), a clearer understanding of the Church will emerge, combined with a deeper, more enlightened appreciation of her ministry. This new understanding and appreciation will be embodied in practice: in the way people use the sacraments and respond to the enfleshed, incarnate teaching and ministry of the Church.

But what can we say in response to the problem now? The key to its solution is to get out of the "getting to heaven" mode of thought. Our goal in embracing Christianity is not just to "get to heaven," any more than our goal in receiving the Sacrament of Reconciliation (as we have tried to explain all through these pages) is just to "get back into the state of grace" or to "get forgiven."

The goal of Jesus Christ in coming to earth was to let us *know the Father and know himself* (Matthew 11:25-30). He came that we might "have life and have it to the full" (John

56

10:10). And he said,

> "Eternal life is this:
> to know you, the only true God,
> and him whom you have sent, Jesus Christ." (John 17:3)

Jesus came so this knowledge of God, this union with the Father, the Son and the Spirit in grace, this interaction with God in human flesh, might enrich our lives and be the fullness of our existence on earth—*now* on earth and forever in heaven.

TO TURN AWAY from this experience, to say that all we are interested in is "getting to heaven" when we die, is to misunderstand (and to reject) Christianity at its core. It is a new gnosticism, a new denial of the physical, incarnate reality of God.

St. John wrote:

> This is how you can recognize God's Spirit:
> every spirit that acknowledges Jesus Christ come in the
> flesh
> belongs to God,
> while every spirit that fails to acknowledge him
> does not belong to God.   (1 John 4:2-3)

Some people—some Catholics—are saying in action, by their failure to deal incarnately with the incarnate Church, that Jesus Christ is no longer present in the flesh. These people are acting as if the physical, embodied presence of God in Jesus and in his Church were not really important. They reduce religion to "getting to heaven." And because this is theoretically possible without conscious and explicit interaction with Jesus in the flesh, they say that relationship with the incarnate Jesus and his incarnate Church is not important.

A turning-away from the Sacrament of Reconciliation

is one of the actions in which this perhaps unconscious, unrecognized new gnosticism surfaces and reveals itself.

In another statement during the Synod, Bishop Vaughan drew the connection between the practice of frequent, private confession and faith in the incarnate reality of Jesus in his Church:

> Every use of the Sacrament of Penance is an implicit acknowledgment and reaffirmation of basic attitudes in Catholic life. Let me just list 10, although there are many more:
>
> 1) Every time I go to confession I implicitly acknowledge that I am a sinner, not just part of a *massa damnata* (a miscellaneous mass of sinners) but with sins of my own that were my own fault.
>
> 2) Every time I go to confession I affirm implicitly that God's mercy is always available to me; that I can never get so far away that he does not care about me; that no sin is unforgivable; that God is a Father who sent his Son to save me by his suffering and death. (This has a special significance in an age when many people wonder if God or anyone else really cares about them.)
>
> 3) Every time I implicitly affirm that God's mercy comes through Christ. The most poorly instructed penitent knows that it is the power of Jesus, not just the priest, who is forgiving his sins.
>
> 4) Every time I implicitly affirm that God's mercy reaches me through the Church, that she is a mother who loves me in this sacrament even when I cannot love myself, and that God himself wants me to come to him by sharing in the Church's life.
>
> 5) Every time I go to confession I reaffirm that a priest is God's minister in a unique way.
>
> 6) Every time I go I implicitly reaffirm that I can do things with God's grace that I will never succeed in doing on my own. Otherwise, sometimes a purpose of amendment would be meaningless.
>
> 7) Every time I implicitly affirm that God wants me to face my sins squarely—say I am sorry for them specifically—and mean it. This means rejecting a part of my past life so that the days ahead can be better than those behind.

8) Every time I implicitly reaffirm that God expects me to do better with and through his grace.

9) Every time I implicitly reaffirm that he wants me to make up for my sins and those of others.

10) Every time a penitent goes to confession he is implicitly drawn to reception of the Eucharist.

In a sense, devotional confession is our need for redemption come alive.

The implicit principle behind all of these statements is that we grow in the "grace of our Lord Jesus Christ" (which we proclaim and rejoice in at the beginning of every Eucharistic celebration) by letting that grace *express itself in and through our human actions*.

Every time that Bishop Vaughan uses the phrase, "I implicitly affirm…" in the passage cited above, he is referring to an action which does not make sense without the act of faith this action expresses. By expressing faith in action, we grow in faith. That is the law of Christian growth.

RECONCILIATION IS a sacrament of growth. It is a sacrament through which we grow into awareness and experience of a truth most vital to our times: the truth that Jesus Christ lives and ministers in his Church, and that we—all of the baptized—are his real Body on earth.

Other books by David Knight

**Living God's Word: Reflections on the Weekly Gospels—
Year A.** ISBN 0-86716-306-2. $14.95

**Living God's Word: Reflections on the Weekly Gospels—
Year B.** ISBN 0-86716-307-0. $14.95

**Living God's Word: Reflections on the Weekly Gospels—
Year C.** ISBN 0-86716-308-9. $14.95

Reaching Jesus: 5 Steps to a Fuller Life.
ISBN 0-86716-296-1. $7.95

Available from
St. Anthony Messenger Press
1615 Republic St.
Cincinnati, OH 45210

call toll-free 1-800-488-0488

email StAnthony@AmericanCatholic.org

order online at www.AmericanCatholic.org